Jolie Blonde
and the Three Héberts

Jolie Blonde
and the Three Héberts
A CAJUN TWIST TO AN OLD TALE

By Sheila Hébert Collins

Illustrated by Patrick Soper

PELICAN PUBLISHING COMPANY

Gretna 1999

This book is dedicated to Irby Hébert, the Papa Hébert of
Cordell, Reid, Byron, Irby Jr., and Sheila.
He is loved and remembered by all as a true Cajun storyteller
and a wonderful papa.

First published by Blue Heron Press, 1993
Revised and published by arrangement with the author by
  Pelican Publishing Company, Inc., 1999

First Pelican edition, 1999

The word "Pelican" and the depiction of a pelican are trademarks
of Pelican Publishing Company, Inc., and are registered in the
U.S. Patent and Trademark Office.

Library of Congress Cataloging-in-Publication Data

Collins, Sheila Hébert.
    Jolie Blonde and the three Héberts : a Cajun twist to an old tale / by
Sheila Hébert Collins ; illustrated by Patrick Soper.
        p.   cm.
    Summary: A Cajun version of "Goldilocks and the Three Bears" featuring
a family named Hébert rather than three bears.
    ISBN 1-56554-324-6 (hardcover : alk. paper)
    [1. Folklore. 2. Cajuns—Folklore.] I. Soper, Patrick, ill. II. Goldilocks
and the three bears. English. III. Title.
PZ8.1.C696Jo 1999
398.2'089'410763—dc21
[E]   98-46397
                                                                          CIP
                                                                           AC

Printed in Hong Kong

Published by Pelican Publishing Company, Inc.
1000 Burmaster Street, Gretna, Louisiana 70053

Jolie Blonde and the Three Héberts

Once upon a time there lived a family of *Héberts*, Mama Hébert, Papa Hébert, and *BéBé* Hébert. They lived on the *bayou* about two miles from *Thibodaux*.

Hébert (AY-bair)—a Cajun family name
BéBé (bay bay)—the baby of the family
bayou (bye-yoo)—a slow-moving stream
Thibodaux (Tib-uh-doh)—a town in South Louisiana

Early one fall evening, Mama Hébert decided to make a good *gumbo*. When it was done, she set it out on the table and said, "Let's go for a *pirogue* ride 'til duh gumbo cools."

gumbo (gum-bo)—a rich Cajun soup served with rice
pirogue (pee-rohg)—a small boat made of cypress

So off they went, down the bayou.

In the town of Thibodaux, right there on the Main Street, there lived a pretty little girl known by all the town as *Jolie Blonde* because of her pretty blond hair. Well, on that very same evening, *petite* Jolie Blonde decided to *rôder* along the bayou.

Jolie Blonde (zho-lee blond)—pretty blonde
petite (p'teet)—small
rôder (ro-DAY)—to travel from place to place

Just about the time she was growing tired, Jolie Blonde saw the Héberts' house, so she decided to stop there to take a little rest and, of course, *veillée* a while.

veillée (vay-yay)—to stay a while and visit in the evening

Jolie Blonde knocked *à la porte*, but no one answered. She opened the door and said, "*Bonjour!* Anyone home?" Again no answer.

à la porte (ah lah port)—at the door
bonjour (bonh-zhoor)—hello

Well, Jolie Blonde couldn't help but smell that good gumbo, and it sure made her hungry. So she followed her nose to the kitchen, where she found three bowls of gumbo—one big one, *gros comme ça,* for Papa, one medium one for Mama, and one little bowl for BéBé.

gros comme ça (gro cuhm sah)—big like that (this saying is accompanied by a hand gesture indicating size)

Jolie Blonde sat down and took a big bite from the big bowl. *"C'est chaud!"* she said. Then she took a bite from the medium bowl and said, *"Mais non! C'est froid!"* Finally, she took a bite from the little bowl and said, "Ummm . . . *ça c'est bon!"* And she ate it all up!

c'est chaud (say sho)—that's hot
mais non! (meh nonh)—oh no!
c'est froid (say fwah)—that's cold
ça c'est bon (sah say bonh)—that is good

That gumbo made Jolie Blonde *fatiguée,* so she went out on the back porch to pass some time in the rocking chair. She found three rocking chairs—one big one, one medium-sized one, and one small one.

fatiguée (fah-tee-GAY)—especially tired

Jolie Blonde sat in the big rocking chair and said, "Mais non, *ça c'est grande!*" Then she tried the medium chair and said, "Dis cushion is too lumpy!" Last she tried the little chair and said, "*C'est bien!* Dis is jus' right!" And she rocked and rocked so much that the rocker broke to the floor.

ça c'est grande (sah say grahnd)—that is big
c'est bien (say byenh)—it's good

By that time Jolie Blonde was *très fatiguée,* so she decided to find a bed and *fais dodo.* Jolie Blonde went upstairs and found three beds—one big one for Papa, one petite one for BéBé, and one *comme-ci, comme-ça* for Mama. She tried Papa's bed and said, "Dis one is too hard." She tried Mama's bed and said, "Dis one is too soft." Last, she tried BéBé's bed and said, "Oh, *yi yi!* Dis is jus' right!"

très fatiguée (tray fah-tee-GAY)—very tired
fais dodo (fay doh-doh)—go to sleep
comme-ci, comme-ça (cuhm-see, cuhm-sah)—a little like this and
  a little like that, meaning not good or bad, but in between
yi yi (y-eye y-eye)—a Cajun expression meaning oh my!

And Jolie Blonde fell asleep, *toute de suite.*

toute de suite (toot sweet)—very quickly

Maintenant, the Héberts came home from their pirogue ride. Well, Papa Hébert went straight to his gumbo and looked at his bowl. "Who's dat been eatin' my gumbo?" he roared.

maintenant (manht-nonh)—now

Mama Hébert looked at her bowl and said, *"Mais, ça quand-même!* Someone's been eatin' my gumbo, too!"

Then BéBé Hébert looked at her gumbo bowl and said, "Whoever dat was ate my gumbo, *c'est parti!"* And she began to cry.

mais, ça quand-même! (meh sah conh-mem)—well, that's some-
thing else!
c'est parti (say pahr-TEE)—it's all gone

"Don't *boudez*, BéBé!" said Mama Hébert. "Let's go rock while I heat some more gumbo."

So they all went out onto the porch. When Papa Hébert got to the porch and saw the rocking chairs, he said, *"Mais, gardez donc ça!* Someone's been rockin' in my chair!"

"In my chair, too, *sha!"* said Mama.

boudez (boo-day)—cry or pout
mais, gardez donc ça (meh gahr-day donh sah)—well, look at that
sha (sha)—darling

Then BéBé cried out, "Someone's been rockin' in my chair, *aussi,* and now it's all broken!"

aussi (oh-SEE)—also

"Don't cry, BéBé. Come on now, let's go *dodo* before you take sick from all dat crying," comforted Mama Hébert.

So, they all went upstairs.

dodo (doh doh)—sleep

When Papa Hébert took one look at his messy bed he was *bien fâché*. "Who's dat been sleepin' in my bed?" he roared.

Mama Hébert looked at her bed and in her most angry voice said, "An' who's dat been sleepin' in my bed?"

bien fâché (byenh fah-SHAY)—very angry

Then BéBé screamed as loud as she could, *"Mon Dieu!* Someone's for sure been sleepin' in my bed, an' dere she is!"

Mama and Papa rushed over to BéBé's bed and they all looked down at Jolie Blonde.

mon Dieu (monh dyu)—my goodness

At just that moment, Jolie Blonde woke up and opened her sleepy eyes. And what did she see? Papa Hébert looking down at her with those big, angry eyes, and . . . *POOH-YI!*

pooh-yi (poo-y-eye)—a Cajun expression meaning oh, my!

She jumped out of that bed, ran out of that house *très vite,* and ran all the way home without looking back once.

très vite (tray veet)—very fast

Today, this same story is told all over the United States. But Jolie Blonde says they tell it all wrong! She says, *"Mais, ces Américains,* dey don't understand about dese Héberts. . . . Dey tink dey are REAL BEARS! Imagine dat!"

mais, ces Américains (meh, say zah-mer-ee-canh)—well, those Americans (Cajuns once referred to anyone who spoke just English as *"Américain"*)

MAMA HEBERT'S GUMBO
(easy enough for any *jolie blonde*)

⅔ cup flour
⅔ cup vegetable oil
1 chopped onion
5 cups water
4 precooked skinless, deboned, cubed chicken breasts coated with salt and cayenne (pre-cook skinless breasts in microwave and save drippings to add to roux)

1 lb. turkey sausage, sliced
1 cup frozen chopped okra (optional)
1 tbsp. Worcestershire sauce
1 tsp. hot sauce
Salt and pepper to taste
¼ cup chopped parsley
6 cups cooked rice

Mais, all gumbo starts with a roux, a cooked flour and oil mixture. Here is how you can make it the easy way.

Mix flour and oil in a 6-cup, microwave-safe measuring cup. Microwave the mixture about 6 minutes on high. Stir. At this time, the roux should be a light brown. Then cook it for 1 minute and stir. Continue this until the roux is the color of a chocolate bar.

Add the onions and microwave for 3 minutes on high. Now you're ready to put the roux into a gumbo pot (*les Américains* may call it a soup pot). Add the water, bring to a boil on the stove, and simmer.

After 15 minutes add the chicken, drippings, sliced sausage, okra if you like, Worcestershire sauce, and hot sauce. Bring to a boil then simmer for 1 hour. Taste to see if you should add salt or pepper.

Sprinkle with parsley and serve over cooked rice in individual gumbo bowls. Don't forget the French bread. *Bon appétit, mes amis!*